# Sending Signals

## Contents

Signals  Can  Be  Seen                                    4

Signals  Can  Be  Heard                                  10

Signals  Can  Be
Seen  and  Heard                                         14

What  Are
These  Signals  Saying?                                  16

We can talk to each other
without using words.
Can you guess how?

## Signals Can Be Seen

Smoke tells us there is a fire.

A lighthouse tells ships
to keep away from rocks.

4

People who are lost
or in danger
use flares to signal for help.

At the airport,
workers signal the pilot
where to move the jet.

6

Traffic lights tell drivers
to stop or go.

Flags can be used to
send messages.

**Signals Can Be Heard**
A train whistles to signal
that it is coming.

The telephone rings
to let us know
someone wants to talk to us.

The alarm clock rings
to let us know
it is time to wake up.

The smoke detector wails
to let us know
there is smoke.

13

## Signals Can Be Seen and Heard

A crosswalk signal
beeps and flashes
to let us know when
to cross the street.

Emergency vehicles
use sirens and lights
to let us know
they are coming.

15

YOUNGSTOWN SCHOOL

# What Are These Signals Saying?